Mummies, Pyramids, and Pharaohs

— A Book about Ancient Egypt —

by GAIL GIBBONS

LITTLE, BROWN AND COMPANY

New York · An AOL Time Warner Company

For Maria Modugno, my editor and friend,
who rode a camel by the pyramids of Egypt

Copyright © 2004 by Gail Gibbons

First Edition

Library of Congress Cataloging-in-Publication Data

Gibbons, Gail.
  Mummies, pyramids, and Pharaohs : a book about ancient Egypt / by Gail Gibbons. —
1st ed.
     p. cm.
  Summary: Provides an overview of life in ancient Egypt, describing the people, daily
activities, beliefs and customs, and what has been learned from artifacts left behind.
  ISBN 0-316-30928-1
    1. Egypt — Civilization — To 332 B.C. — Juvenile literature. [1. Egypt — Civilization — To
332 B.C.] I. Title.

DT61 .G52 2003
932 — dc21

2002022560

10 9 8 7 6 5 4 3 2 1

Book design by Saho Fujii

TWP

Printed in Singapore

The illustrations for this book were done in watercolors.
The text was set in Legacy and Galahad, and the display type is Papyrus.

PHARAOH

One of the world's oldest continuous civilizations began about five thousand years ago, in the land of Egypt. For the next three thousand years the Egyptians were ruled by kings called pharaohs. While he was in power, each pharaoh was believed to be Horus, the son of the great sun god, Re.

The ancient Egyptians lived in northeast Africa along the Nile River. They called the dark and fertile soil around the Nile the "Black Land" and used it for growing their crops.

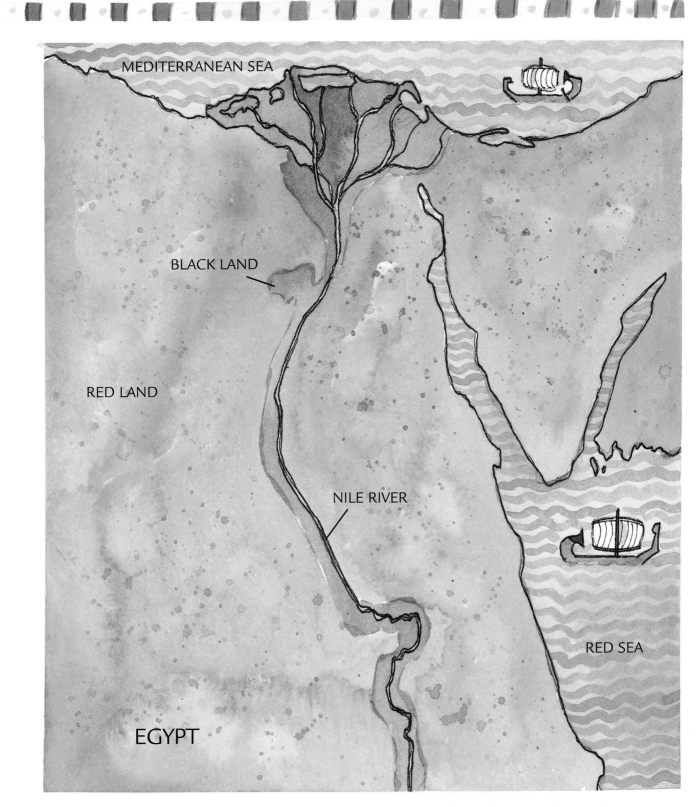

MEDITERRANEAN SEA

BLACK LAND

RED LAND

NILE RIVER

RED SEA

EGYPT

Beyond the dark soil was what the Egyptians called the "Red Land." It was a huge, stony, red desert area where it rarely rained and few plants grew.

The pharaohs built Egypt into a rich and powerful nation. When a pharaoh died, his son inherited the throne. The wives of pharaohs were powerful, too, although only a few women ever ruled Egypt.

The royal couple often appeared in processions and celebrations, and took trips to the temples to worship their many gods. The pharaoh's family dressed in rich fabrics decorated with gold and precious stones to display its wealth and power.

The CHIEF MINISTER was in charge of taxes and the overseeing of crops and irrigation. He also acted as the pharaoh's lawyer and settled disputes.

MONARCHS were in charge of different regions of Egypt.

The TEMPLE PRIEST held religious ceremonies.

Ancient Egyptian society was highly organized. There were the very honored people.

Most people worked for the pharaoh and the kingdom as craftspeople, farmers, or laborers. There were also soldiers, as well as slaves who had been captured during wars.

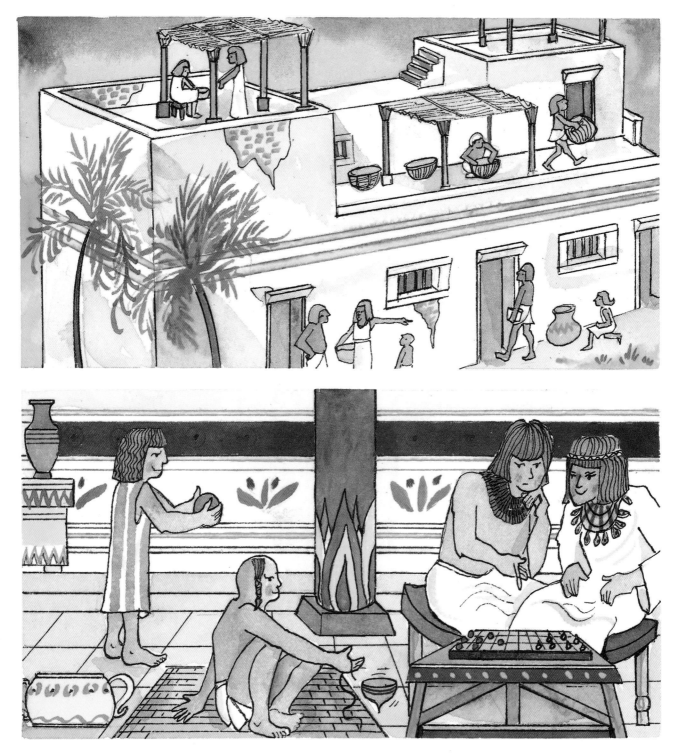

Most families lived in villages of sunbaked mud houses set close together. The houses had few windows, flat roofs, and square rooms with very little furniture. Wealthy families had servants and lived surrounded by beautiful objects.

Ancient Egyptians loved perfumes. They rubbed scented oils on their skin to protect themselves from the dry climate, too.

Because of the heat, ancient Egyptians wore light linen clothing. Most of the time the fabric was white. Slaves and servants, who came from foreign lands, wore patterned fabrics. Everyone cared greatly about how they looked. Men and women, both rich and poor, owned jewelry and used makeup, especially eye paint.

Farmers depended on water from the Nile to grow their crops. During the growing season canals carried water to the fields. This is called irrigation. The farmers grew barley, wheat, fruit, and vegetables. Farmers also raised livestock such as water buffalo, cattle, sheep, and goats for food.

Egyptian paintings told stories about living people, and also about what they hoped to see when they died and met their gods.

The craftspeople included potters, carpenters, glassmakers, leather workers, jewelers, and weavers. Copper and gold were plentiful in Egypt and were used in many art forms.

The ROSETTA STONE was the key to modern scholars' understanding of Egyptian picture writing. Because it was written both in hieroglyphs and in Greek, historians were able to learn details of the religion, laws, and everyday lives of ancient Egyptians.

The ROSETTA STONE was found in 1799 by a French soldier near the Egyptian village of Rosetta.

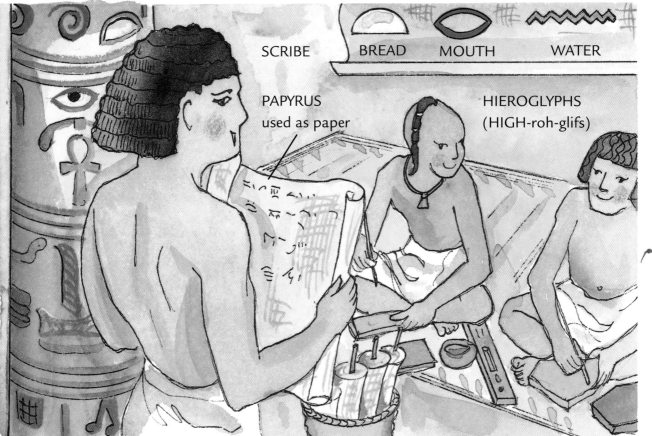

SCRIBE BREAD MOUTH WATER

PAPYRUS
used as paper

HIEROGLYPHS
(HIGH-roh-glifs)

Ancient Egyptians used picture writing. The inscriptions they made on temples and tombs are now known as hieroglyphs. People called scribes spent up to ten years to learn the hundreds of hieroglyph symbols.

AMULETS
(AM-yoo-lets)

RENEWED LIFE

SIGN OF LIFE

INFINITY

PROTECTIVE EYE OF HORUS

PROTECTION FROM WATER DANGERS

PROTECTION FROM HOUSEHOLD ACCIDENTS

Ancient Egyptians believed in medicinal healing and magic. The doctors thought that the heart controlled everything in the body. Plants, such as garlic, were used as medicines. When medicine didn't work, doctors tried magic. They often used lucky charms, called amulets, and believed their gods had healing powers.

The pharaoh and his family often put on great feasts and celebrations with dancers, storytellers, musicians, and other entertainers. They served tasty foods and drinks. It was a time of merriment.

Poorer people held celebrations at their yearly harvests and religious festivals. There was music, dancing, and garlands of flowers.

The HIGH PRIEST and the PHARAOH were the only ones allowed in the inner sanctuary.

The ancient Egyptians worshipped many gods. Many pharaohs had temples built in honor of themselves and their gods. These huge temples contained large statues, massive columns, workshops, gardens, and a place of worship called the inner sanctuary.

Every town or settlement had its own temple for its local god or family of gods. Each day the priests took the statues, washed them, dressed them, offered them food, and placed them back on their shrines.

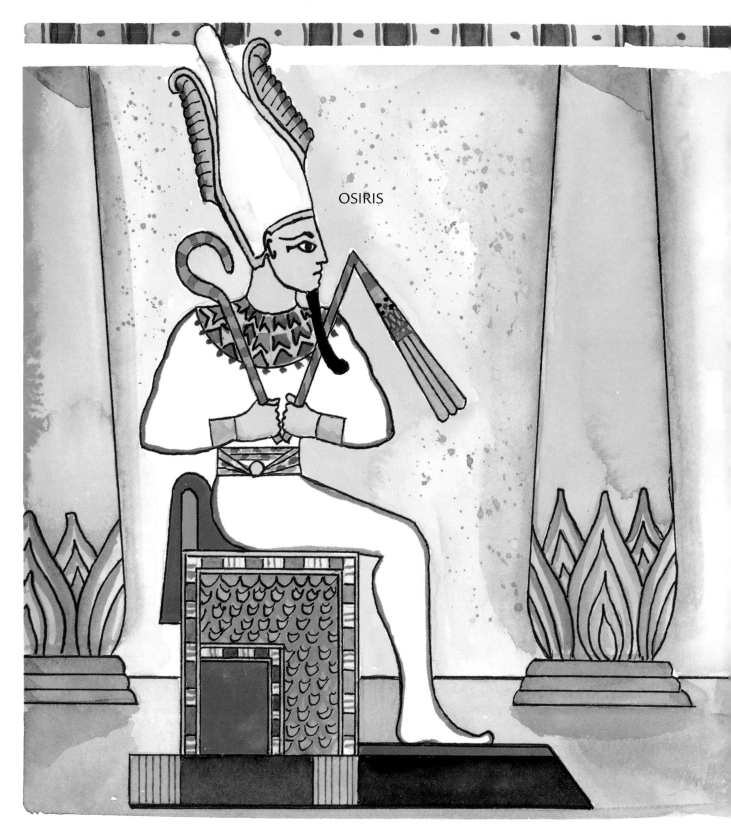

OSIRIS

Ancient Egyptians believed in life after death, called the afterlife. Osiris (o-SYE-rus) was the god of the underworld. The Egyptians also believed every person had two important parts.

The bird of Ba united the Ka and the Ba.

KA

BA

The "Ka" was the life force. The "Ba" was the person's soul. In order to live forever in the afterlife, the Ka and the Ba had to be united. The body of a dead person had to be preserved for the afterlife.

EMBALMING PRIESTS

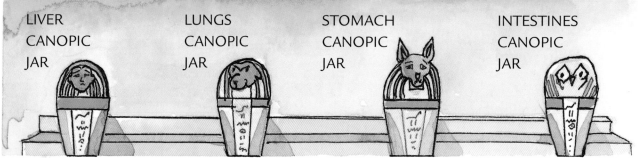

LIVER
CANOPIC
JAR

LUNGS
CANOPIC
JAR

STOMACH
CANOPIC
JAR

INTESTINES
CANOPIC
JAR

Pharaohs and their families and noblemen had elaborate burials involving mummification. It was believed that when a pharaoh died he became a god. Embalming priests prepared the pharaoh's body for the afterlife. First, the body's organs were removed. Some of them were placed in their own special jars, called canopic (can-OH-pick) jars. Only the heart was left inside the body.

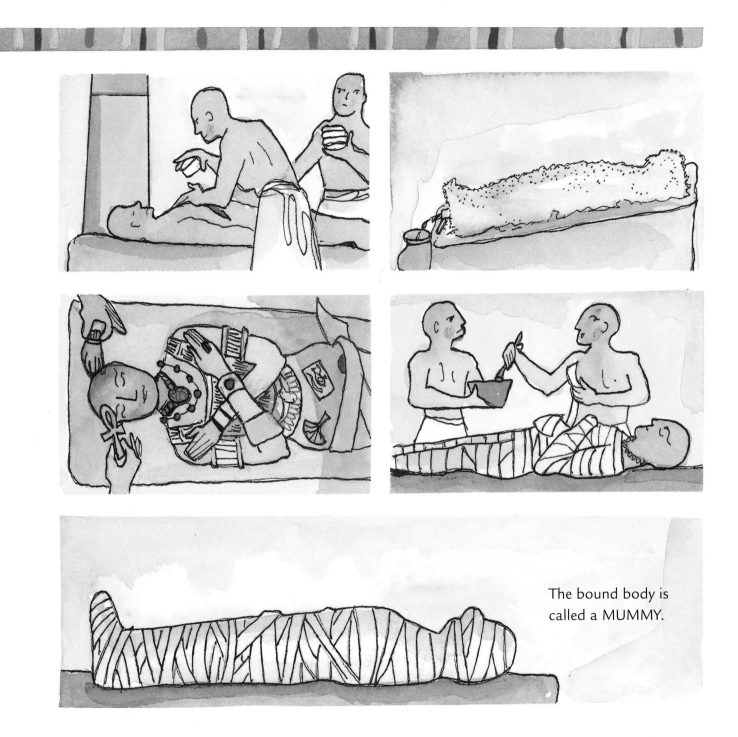

The bound body is called a MUMMY.

Cloth was stuffed inside the body. Then the skin was covered with a chemical to dry the body out. After forty days the chemical was removed. Then the body was covered with oils, precious stones, and amulets. Next, it was bound with long strips of cloth over and over again. A highly decorated mask was placed over the face, and the body was wrapped once again. The entire process took about seventy days.

The mummy was placed in a coffin, or sometimes a series of coffins. A funeral procession brought the mummy to a great tomb called a pyramid out in the red land, the desert.

PYRAMID

The pyramid was a huge four-sided structure, built as a monument to the pharaoh. It took thousands of stone workers and artists their lifetime — and millions of stone blocks — to complete one.

Food, tools, jewelry, and other beloved things were placed next to a body for its afterlife in the kingdom of Osiris.

SARCOPHAGUS
(sar-COFF-uh-gus)

Inside the pyramid was the pharaoh's burial chamber. The interior walls were covered with magnificent carvings and paintings. Then the coffin was placed inside a large stone box called a sarcophagus.

Figurines of servants, called SHABTI, were buried along with the dead to serve in the afterlife.

Many of the pharaoh's possessions and treasures were placed in the pyramid for the afterlife. The canopic jars, guarded by their own gods, were placed in a chest nearby.

Inside the pyramid, near the pharaoh's burial chamber, were temples, storage chambers, and burial chambers for royal family members and servants.

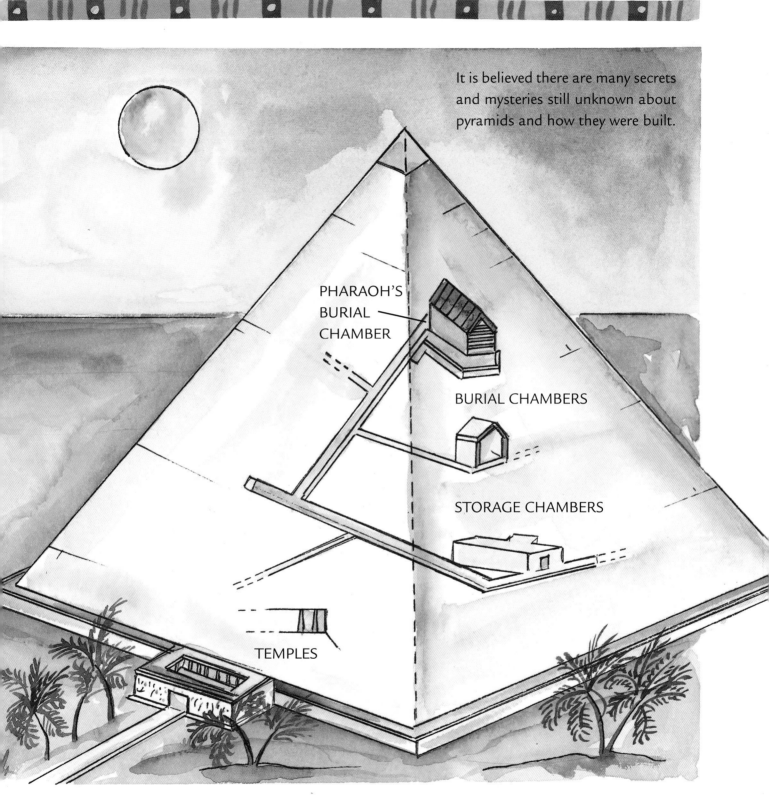

It is believed there are many secrets and mysteries still unknown about pyramids and how they were built.

PHARAOH'S BURIAL CHAMBER

BURIAL CHAMBERS

STORAGE CHAMBERS

TEMPLES

When the procession left, the entrance to the pyramid was sealed up. Stone slabs were put into place. The pharaoh was in his final resting place before going on to his afterlife.

THE PYRAMIDS AND
THE SPHINX AT GIZA

Today, after thousands of years, these great pyramids still exist. Many travelers go to see them. These people feel in touch with the grand and fascinating era of the ancient Egyptians.

Many museums around the world display beautiful pieces of ancient Egyptian art and architecture. In some exhibits mummies are seen. The ancient Egyptians had one powerful wish, the wish to live forever in their afterlives.

ANCIENT EGYPT DISCOVERIES . . .

An Egyptologist studies ancient Egyptian history.

Some people think the shapes of Egypt and its stretch of the Nile look like a lotus plant, with the Nile as the stem and the delta as the flower.

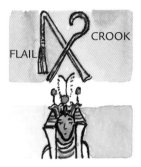

The pharaoh held a crook and flail, symbols of power that linked him to the god Osiris.

When Queen Hatshepsut's husband died, she ruled Egypt for about twenty years.

More than eighty pyramids have been discovered in Egypt.

The first pyramid was built for King Zoser. It was called a step pyramid because of its shape. Later, step pyramids changed to become flat-sided pyramids.

Khufu's Great Pyramid, the biggest of three massive pyramids at Giza, is the largest in Egypt. It stands 479 feet (146 meters) tall and contains over two million blocks of limestone. It took about 100,000 men over twenty years to build it.

A pyramid-shaped capstone went on the top of many pyramids. Egyptologists believe the three Giza capstones were covered with gold.

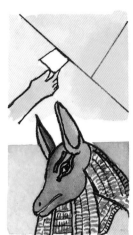

Measurements were very precise for the building of the ancient Egyptian pyramids. A piece of paper cannot be pushed between the stone slabs.

The priest in charge of making a mummy wore the mask of a jackal, which symbolized Anubis, the god of the dead and mummification.

Massive stone monuments stood guard over the great pyramids. The Sphinx is a huge statue with the head of a pharaoh and the body of a lion. The pharaoh symbolized leadership and the lion stood for power.

Ancient Egyptians had their own style of art. When they drew people and animals, they drew front and side views. The artists thought this gave the best perspective of what they were drawing.

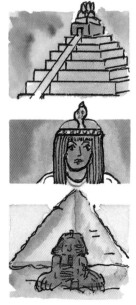

Other cultures, like the Mayans and the Aztecs, built great pyramids, too. They were shaped and decorated differently than Egyptian pyramids.

Cleopatra was the seventh and last Greek pharaoh. She knew the Egyptian language.

Although moisture, wind, sandstorms, and tourists have damaged many of the pyramids over time, they still tell us much about the ideas and beliefs of the people who built them.